CALLINGS

ALSO BY CARL DENNIS

POETRY

A House of My Own
Climbing Down
Signs and Wonders
The Near World
The Outskirts of Troy
Meetings with Time
Ranking the Wishes
Practical Gods
New and Selected Poems 1974–2004
Unknown Friends

PROSE

Poetry as Persuasion

CALLINGS

Carl Dennis

PENGUIN POETS

PENGUIN BOOKS
Published by the Penguin Group
Penguin Group (USA) Inc., 375 Hudson Street, New York, New York 10014, U.S.A.
Penguin Group (Canada), 90 Eglinton Avenue East, Suite 700, Toronto, Ontario,
Canada M4P 2Y3 (a division of Pearson Penguin Canada Inc.)
Penguin Books Ltd, 80 Strand, London WC2R 0RL, England
Penguin Ireland, 25 St Stephen's Green, Dublin 2, Ireland
(a division of Penguin Books Ltd)
Penguin Group (Australia), 250 Camberwell Road, Camberwell, Victoria 3124,
Australia (a division of Pearson Australia Group Pty Ltd)
Penguin Books India Pvt Ltd, 11 Community Centre,
Panchsheel Park, New Delhi - 110 017, India
Penguin Group (NZ), 67 Apollo Drive, Rosedale,
North Shore 0632, New Zealand (a division of Pearson New Zealand Ltd)
Penguin Books (South Africa) (Pty) Ltd, 24 Sturdee Avenue,
Rosebank, Johannesburg 2196, South Africa

Penguin Books Ltd, Registered Offices:
80 Strand, London WC2R 0RL, England

First published in Penguin Books 2010

1   3   5   7   9   10   8   6   4   2

Page ix constitutes an extension of this copyright page.

LIBRARY OF CONGRESS CATALOGING-IN-PUBLICATION DATA
Dennis, Carl.
Callings / Carl Dennis.
p. cm.
ISBN 978-0-14-311838-1
I. Title.
PS3554.E535C35 2010
811'.54—dc22   2010025511

Printed in the United States of America
Set in Sabon
Designed by Sabrina Bowers

for Tony Hoagland

Acknowledgments

Thanks are due to the editors of the following magazines, in which some of these poems first appeared:

American Poetry Review, "Belittle," "Drugstore," and
    "Pioneers"
The Atlantic Monthly, "Dancers"
Cerise Press, "A Roofer," "Style," and "Tribal"
Five Points, "Mission to Ganymede" and "Other Options"
The Greensboro Review, "To the Angel of Death"
Gulf Coast, "Tattoo"
The Kenyon Review, "A Word from the Sleepless"
Meridian, "Praise"
Mid American Review, "Leonardo" and "Warning Signs"
The Nation, "A Realtor"
The Ohio Review, "The Mood" and "Recall Notice"
Ploughshares, "Devising Scripture" and "Disgust"
Poetry, "Silent Prophet"
Poetry Northwest, "Ants"
Salmagundi, "After the Second Flood," "The Best World," and
    "Normal"
Southern Poetry Review, "Anthropology"

I would also like to thank the generous friends who gave me valuable criticism on all these poems: Charles Altieri, Thomas Centolella, Alan Feldman, Mark Halliday, Tony Hoagland, Martin Pops, and Philip Schultz.

"Praise" is for Catherine Barnett.
"Belittle" is for Thomas Centolella.
"Instructions from Lucy in Elmira" is for Alan Feldman.
"More Poetry" is for Martin Pops.
"To the Angel of Death" is for Philip Schultz.

Contents

CALLINGS

Other Options

No open land now, no freedom to practice
The first of the callings, hunting and gathering.
Still, the settlements have brought other options:
Openings for a blacksmith, a cashier, a dentist,
A forklift driver, a logo designer.
As for the young clerk in the garden store
At West Ferry and Grant who's had to put off
His plan to become a forester, maybe he'll save enough
In a year or two for a forestry program
If he chooses to live now like a monk.
And I can add a woman I know well,
A teacher of ecology at City Honors,
Who once was troubled to think a career in music
Might have been hers if she'd started lessons earlier
And proved more fervent. Now she's content
To rest after school while Chopin's mazurkas
Or Schubert's impromptus waft from the stereo,
Cheered by the zeal of someone determined
To keep alive the vocation she didn't choose.
Maybe this evening she'll listen a little longer
To mark the end of the five-week unit
Showing how a strong defense of the biosphere
Is in harmony with a strong economy.
Though few of her students may choose her field,
It's enough if they understand why others
Might find the work engrossing.
The options are more than ample,
And she doesn't divide them into high and low.
She agreed when I argued that maintaining a list
Of all the callings available might itself
Prove a useful calling, assigning a name

To many choices not named before.
And I agreed with her when she suggested
That simply listening to Chopin or Schubert
Might be a calling for the few possessed
Of a dedication that's undivided,
Who bring as much as they take away.

At the Wine Store

He's a man whose words are few and measured,
The owner of the wine store at Hodge and Elmwood,
Who, when he pronounces a bottle "fine,"
Means neither that it's merely decent
Nor that it's so superb it can turn a day
One hopes to forget into a day
One hopes to recall long afterward.
He means if you're looking for something
To serve at a dinner welcoming home
A friend after an absence of many months,
This bottle won't disappoint you.
"Fine," implying the wine's too grand
To be drunk by yourself unless you're moved
To raise a glass to your lucky stars.
A toast, say, on the day you learn, after tests,
That the lingering pain in your side
Is nothing serious. A fine day,
You'll say to yourself as you step
From the clinic into a street
That appears in your hour-long absence
To have been washed by a yearlong rain
More cleansing than any you've known before.
In such a mood this bottle will prove so fitting
You'll raise a glass to the vintner's husbandry
And to whatever his parents did to encourage
His loyalty to the highest standards.
And why not a toast to the village women
You can imagine as barefoot girls
Treading the grapes in a giant tub?
They'll all be here in the first sip—
That's the unstated guarantee

Implied by the owner's terse endorsement.
A fine bottle that shows how open you are
To the gifts that sun and soil unite to offer,
How keen to enjoy them when they pass your way.

Tribal

Tribal music is throbbing tonight from River Records
As I leave the warmth of the Hunan Kitchen
And make my way along snow-struck Niagara Street.
A heavy drumbeat that might have prompted
Even the tribal elders to join the dance.
It follows me, fading, as I follow the smoke
Of my own breath the few blocks to my car.
Nobody out braving the cold tonight,
Unless I count the man bedded down
In the dark doorway of Safeway Appliances.
For a moment, the inch-thick blanket of snow
Flung over him and his cart seems to translate him
Into a marble monument to an unknown refugee
Whose tribal village had to be abandoned.
Maybe its well dried up.
Maybe it was torched by soldiers or gangs.
Here, he sleeps by the roadside. There,
He'd be cozy under his own roof
With his wife and children, or lodged as a guest
With a family inspired by the tribal doctrine
That regards the roofless as god-protected.
If this night turns out as cold as predicted,
A van on the prowl may cart him down
To the homeless shelter. As I pass him,
My wish that he wake up rested
Leaves nothing changed. When I reach my car,
It's the work of a moment to brush the snow off
And ease out into the trickle of late-night traffic
With "It's Only a Paper Moon" on the golden-oldies station
For company. Back in the thirties, when this song was new,
A man like the sleeper might have ridden the rails
With a tribe of nomads looking for work.

Now he's simply someone soon to wake up
To the chilly fact he lacks an address
And isn't likely to find one.
If better fortune finds him, it will take the form
Of someone enrolled in a tribe I don't belong to,
Bound by a code I have no trouble
Admiring from a distance as suiting
The gifts of its eager adherents exactly.
For people like that, such kindness comes naturally,
I tell myself. For me to attempt it
I'd have to pretend to be someone else.

Rescue

Those few who ride off in search of the truth
And are lucky enough to come across it
After years of wandering
Are likely to settle down on the spot
And bask in its steady brightness.
For them to trudge back to the dark for us,
Some motive other than love of the truth
Must also be working,
One they may not be able to name,
One they may try to resist
Even at the moment they reach the ridge
Overlooking the cluster of tattered tents
That make up our camp in the wilderness.
How tempting for them to gaze down on us
As we might gaze down from a seat
In the balcony on a character
Doomed by his ignorance and impulsiveness,
And by the plot of the play he stars in,
To make the same blunder he always makes.
Truth declares Othello's downfall predictable
Ten minutes after the curtain opens.
Some other voice will have to prompt us
If we're to be moved to descend to the stage
And act the part of a friend not provided,
Of counterpoise to the secret enemy.
Now to urge the hero to pause a moment,
Listen, and reconsider. Now to assure him
He needn't always stumble without a candle
To the final scene, needn't always learn late
What he'd give everything to learn earlier.

Silent Prophet

It's the last day, but I'm keeping the news to myself.
If yesterday it made sense for letter carriers
To carry letters from door to door,
The job still ought to be worth doing.
Why tell what I know and risk a walkout?
Let firefighters race to the last fire.
Let platoons of police set up their last lines
So the factions that come to the demonstration
Fight only in words and gestures.

The day is different, but only for me,
Knowing as I do there won't be others,
That the world is destined to end at midnight.
It's now or never for a cautious investor
To resist his nature enough
To back a grocery in a battered district.
Now or never for the would-be grocer
To open a bottle of good champagne
In the kitchen of the friend who's led him
Through the small-print maze of the application.
And now—while they're toasting the months to come
Scheduled to move the project along
From drawing blueprints to cutting ribbons—
Shall I tell them their expectations are dreams?

Though silent, I'm rooting for them to let the day
Expand to include the days to be denied them,
Just as I'm rooting for the woman across the hall
From the friend's apartment, who's learning
To play the viola from scratch. Good for her
If she finds an hour today for practice despite
The extra hours required at the insurance firm

As tax day approaches, and the usual work
Of tending two teenage sons alone.

Should I sit on a stone and lament
That this day is her last when I believe
It may well contain, scrolled up within it,
All the years she'll need to play
As she'd like to play, voicing on strings
The feelings stirred by the gap
Between the world she planned to live in
And the world available?

Another prophet, one convinced that the present
Requires the future to give it substance,
May decide to speak out. I'm keeping silent
As one of her sons sits at his desk
Dividing a page into reasons for leaving home
And reasons for staying. It's his last chance
To ask what region has the most to teach him
Or what region will likely prove most in need
Of whatever he'll have to offer
After he learns where his talents lie.

Letter from a Senior Secretary at Potomac School

I'd like to admit at the outset that the job we advertised
In American history might have been yours
If your application hadn't been misfiled,
As sometimes happened under our old procedures.
Under the new, I wouldn't have had to type
The letter sent you last month by the principal
To explain that our opening was already filled.
Then you wouldn't have made your angry phone call,
Which I hope you'll be relieved to know
I didn't mention to him. His cool tone
Wasn't meant to suggest indifference.
It's a tone our lawyers advise, to help us avoid
Conceding so much it leads to litigation,
A problem I'm not concerned with,
Being only three months away from retirement.
Here in this unofficial letter from me,
Which I'm asking you to keep confidential,
I want to point out that wherever you end up teaching
You'll have to learn how to deal with disappointment.
What will you do, say, when the textbook
Chosen by a committee in your new department
Turns out to be shallow as well as slipshod?
Will you look for another job, or will you
Use the occasion to show your students
How to spot the issues the book's neglected
And go looking elsewhere for enlightenment?
If I did my job by the book, I wouldn't have stayed
Late at the office this afternoon to write you this.
I'd have written you off as one of the self-absorbed
Caught up in avenging slights to his dignity.
Keep in mind I could be at home now,

Enjoying a taste for serious fiction and poetry
Passed on to me by my English teacher in high school,
Harriet Henderson. But here I am, extending myself
Beyond the call of duty. Now it's up to you
To ignore or appreciate my extra effort,
Just as the extra effort I hope you make
May or may not impress your students.
Even the best of them, remember,
May not be aware how much they're learning.
So you may not be aware how much these words,
Which now may seem addressed to someone
Dreamed up by me out of nothing,
May later seem to be meant for you.

Pioneers

If time were in fact like money,
We could bank a day like this one
That as yet we have no plans for
And spend it later when we were ready,
Along with any interest that's piled up.
Instead, we're obliged to live it now.
Should we break it down, as we've done
With other days, into desk work and yard work,
Supper and post-supper pastimes,
Or devote it all to making a plan
For one bold enterprise that begins tomorrow?
What would that be exactly? Something more,
It would seem, than merely doing the old work
With a better attitude. Why can't this day
Be like the one our predecessors devoted
To outfitting a wagon train and heading off
Toward the lush land of the middle border?
How easy then to prove we're making progress
When another evening means another inch
Marked on the map from here to there.
No need to rush so long as our pace
Is steady, allowing us to arrive
Before the trail is obscured by snow,
The grass buried too deep for the oxen.
Time then to unload our wagons and marvel
How many items have come through intact,
Though an heirloom bowl has a hairline crack
Running rim to rim. However lonely we feel
As the wind ruffles the tall grass, we'll agree
The spot should begin to feel like home
After a little labor, a little time.
Then we'll drink a toast to the day long gone

When our journey began, the one that now
We're letting slip through our fingers
Here where we can't postpone it.
If anyone claims the loss isn't real,
Let him step forward now.
Let him try to convince us time is a well
Dug in our own yard and always brimming,
However often we dip our cup.

When I Listened

When I listened to the debate on the radio,
I could hear my candidate dismantling one by one
The arguments his opponents raised against him.
But later, when I watched the rerun on TV,
He seemed to falter, so little does good sense
Count for the eye, so easily is the eye
Distracted by a squint or a shaky smile.
No wonder the goddess Justice wears a blindfold.
No other way for her to concentrate
On the issue before her, whether the alibi
Offered by the defendant holds tight
When prodded and jabbed by questions.
Maybe the jury should listen from behind a screen,
As is now the standard procedure in orchestras
When a candidate for an opening
Competes at the final trial.
Who cares if the musician is young or old,
Male or female, well dressed or ragged,
So long as the playing is passionate and insightful.
Just the candidate's voice, then, not his image,
Once the listeners can rid themselves
Of any lingering prejudice against an accent
Or dialect, twang or drawl. If they can't,
Let all the speeches be read on the radio
By a neutral party, assuming each speech
Is composed by the candidate only,
Not by his handlers.
Someone who's thought this through
Must help with the details so the plan
Can be put into action soon. While I wait,
I could work at making my eyes more reliable.
Maybe I'll learn something this afternoon

From the talk at the art museum on how to tell
Which artist is only bluffing and which
Answers the question of how the world
Ought to be viewed when the light is ample,
The world here now or on its way.

Warning Signs

Neatness isn't a virtue to be disparaged.
But if you note that your ten-year-old
Prints her address in her storybooks
As well as her name, and locks her toys
In her toy chest at bedtime,
You may have a problem. Can you think
Of something you've done to suggest
That the world beyond the door of her bedroom
Is a wilderness of swirling eddies
Where anything left untended goes missing?
Has a remark of yours about thieves
Filling high places left her concerned
About thieves filling the low as well?
When she wakes before dawn with a dream
Of finding the house pulled down,
Do you tell her everyone feels that way,
Given the gang of wreckers in Washington,
Or do you remind her that the house she lives in
Is made of bricks and mortar, not straw?

As for the virtue of thrift, it too
Is commendable. But if your daughter
Is saving half her dollar-a-day allowance
So as not to be penniless in old age,
You may want to ask what part you've played
In making the future appear less promising
Than the past. Maybe you've lectured her
Once too often on the long-term effects
Of nitrogen runoff on lakes and rivers,
Or on the threat to the Norway maple
Shading the house if warmer winters
Smooth the way for weevils to creep north.

Other fathers might use the tree as a fine example
Of what a maple can be when it makes the most
Of an average portion of sun and rain
Falling on average soil.

Caution should be preferred, of course, to recklessness.
But confidence too is a trait to be encouraged,
So when she's old she can look back on her life
As an adventure. So she has a story to tell
Of how once, instead of hugging the shore,
She sailed out where the waves
Crashed over her sloop and broke it open;
How the coast she floated to on a spar
Proved rougher than the coast she'd been steering for,
Less settled, less civil. And then the story
Of how far she progressed in her efforts
At closing the gap between them
And how big a job is left to do.

A Roofer

Down on the ground, it's hard for him to measure
How well he's doing, whether he's liable, say,
To be too quick when correcting his children
Or too slow, too distant or too intrusive.
And is honesty what he needs more of
For his wife to be happier, or forbearance?
But on the roof he knows exactly
What the situation requires
And how best to supply it,
Sustained as he is by the clear consensus
Of the ghosts of the great roofers of yesteryear,
Who nod their approval at work well done.

On the ground, as he walks from his job,
He has to be a witness to shoddy craftsmanship:
Potholes gaping again after a month or two,
Porches rebuilt last summer already listing.
And then the boarded windows of the bank
That gambled away the savings of the thrifty.
But on the roof the only work he observes
Is his own of yesterday and the day before,
Good work that inspires him once again
To set his shingles neatly in courses,
Each as secure as nails can make it.

How gently the morning light
Glances along the ladder
As it rises from the world of obscure beginnings
And obscure procedures to the luminous realm
Where the rows of shingles
Climb from drip edge to roof beam
With a logic that's irresistible.

As long as the light holds,
It's a pleasure to linger here
Where he can believe himself an agent of progress.
No need to rush. Already at hand,
The last shingle the job requires
Waits to sit snug in its proper place.

Style

If you haven't time to transform yourself,
You may have enough to fashion a style
For something basic you've done so far
Without any deliberation, like breathing.
It may make a difference, when you stand
At an open window, if you choose to avoid
The small, quick breaths that suggest a fear
Of alien influence. Fill your lungs slowly
And deeply, and maybe you'll sense
Beneath the layered aroma of tar,
Pine, industrial solvents, and grass
A faint, polleny whiff from a tree you feel
Might teach you something important
If you encountered it more directly.
It's a leap of faith to believe you'll find it
On your evening walk when even its name
Keeps to the shadows. Still, your prospects,
However limited, ought to improve
If you make adjustments in your style of walking.
No more shuffling, eyes on the ground,
As if you're convinced luck is against you.
No more rushing, eyes straight ahead,
As if you're afraid of missing
A once-in-a-lifetime performance.
The tree may reveal itself to you
Whenever you're ready to slow your pace
And come to a pause and look around.
Now to admire how its slender trunk
And filigree canopy befit its subtle fragrance,
Or how its shaggy bark and heavy branches
Provide its fragrance a homely foil.
Never mind that it inherits its style

Complete from eons of ancestors while you
Piece yours together by trial and error.
Learn to take pleasure in the effort itself,
And you won't be sorry if you can't step back
Far enough from your handiwork to see it whole.

Leonardo

We say we could use a voice from above
To tell us how well we're doing.
But if it gave us unqualified commendation,
We might be skeptical. And if it ventured
On stern advice about mending our ways,
We might resist it, covertly if not openly,
If we hadn't already come on our own
To the same conclusion. Even if it urged us
To lavish more of our time on whatever
We most love doing, we might demur.
It's hard to believe that if an angel had come
In a dream to Leonardo, enjoining him
To complete more paintings, he'd have decided
To abridge his studies in anatomy and hydraulics,
Optics and metallurgy and the origins of clouds.
The issue isn't only which interest
Is going to prove the most productive;
It's also his effort to be Leonardo,
A man of many interests, not merely one.
It feels presumptuous to label irrelevant
His lifelong interest in birds, which led him
To work near the end on the problem of human flight,
To sketch ingenious devices to get us airborne.
Yes, if a voice from above could speak for us,
It might inform him that with time so scarce
Flight ought to serve him more as a metaphor
For all he can do in his painting,
For soaring in spirit to an ampler perspective
Than the flesh can climb to on its own.
But why can't the flesh and spirit,
He might have asked, go soaring together
For at least a moment? And we'd have to agree

A flight like that might be a pleasure to both,
However galling the tie that bound them
Might sometimes prove after they touched down.

Normal

This time around you're a man who hears
In the word "normal" an undertone of reproof.
But next time it may sound like a blessing,
As soothing a word as it is to someone
Who wakes between cool sheets
After weeks of fever.
All he wants to do is sit in his yard
On a morning like this one, no fresher
Than a normal October morning,
And watch as a squirrel no grayer
Than the one before you darts up the sycamore.
Can you see yourself there as well,
On a bench in a drift of leaves whose reds
And yellows are normal for this time of year?
This time around the figure who sits there
Seems to suffer from a want of will,
A tendency to settle for whatever's offered.
Next time he may seem a hero
For taking pleasure in raking leaves into piles
No higher than those his neighbors make,
At a pace no faster. Plenty of time to finish
Before evening arrives, before a sunset
That won't have to best the others
To be a good one. Plenty even if Chowder
Keeps charging the piles and burrowing in.
A good game, good frisking. Good dog,
Good dog. Now his bark is distracting
As you muse on what's left to be done
If you're to exercise more of your powers
By nightfall. Then it may seem to enhance
The leisurely pace of the moment,
The bark of a farm dog from across the pasture,

Reminding you that you're not required
To add more acres to those you have,
Just to keep plowing when it's time to plow
And harvesting in harvest season
As farmers have always done.

Dancers

At least one couple tonight at the Topaz Room
May have quarreled on the long drive over in the rain
About whether moving to a drier climate
And making new friends would brighten their outlook.
Still they agree, for this evening at least,
That dancing is something they're willing to try.
Maybe tonight, for once, they'll be able to feel
What they'd like to feel: that moving to music
Is an instance, not merely a metaphor,
Of life lived as it should be lived.
Other dancers may be more graceful,
But among the clumsy these two may have learned
To look at their feet without embarrassment.
And if they can't set aside all their differences,
Maybe they can agree tonight that consensus
Is the wrong model for them, too close
For comfort in their private commonwealth
To one-party rule, to tyranny. A dance they enjoy
Won't prove that division is far behind them,
Just that they're making their peace with it
As one defers when the other decides
The tune has come from afar to find them
Here where they ought to be, in the Topaz Room,
Taking one step forward, one step back.

Honesty

All he can think of doing to counter the lies
Officials have fallen back on to explain the war
Is to insist on honesty in the private realm,
Beginning with telling himself the truth
About what moved him, two years ago,
To volunteer three afternoons a week
At the homeless shelter.

Yes, he wanted to give something back
To the town that gave him his friends
And to fill the void opened by his retirement.
But would he have lasted more than a month
If the shelter hadn't also offered the chance
To talk with Maria Finley, the head counselor?

And then to admit he can't be sure
As to the nature of her appeal.
It may be the pleasure she takes in her job:
Pointing clients to options in life they'd assumed
Beyond them. It may be her being younger
By twenty years, her slender figure,
Good posture, and graceful carriage.

And then to recognize he's pretending
To be more moved by the plight of the homeless
Than he actually feels in order to please her,
To induce her to think of him as a soul mate.
At least his feelings for her are genuine,
He tells himself. At least there's a chance

She'd be better off with someone like him,
More taken with her than with her causes.

And now that he's made some headway
In the matter of honesty with himself,
What about taking the next step
And being honest enough with her
To suggest, if she shows some interest,
He's not exactly the man he seems,
Not endowed with so large a spirit.

For that disclosure, he's going to need
More courage than he's needed so far,
Or at least more faith that a flow of truthfulness
In a time of lies is always welcome,
However long it's been delayed.

A Realtor

If the client who bought the mansion had asked her
For her opinion, she believes she might have told him,
Despite the risk to her commission,
That the house seemed too much for a single person
Closer by far to his end than to his beginning.

If he'd asked her, she might have asked him
If he was planning to marry a widow
With seven children or was feeling a sudden need
To entertain on a scale far more lavish
Than any he'd ever practiced before.

If the answer was no, she might have suggested
He'd be better off with the bungalow on her list
In a neighborhood just as stable, priced to sell quickly.
She might have hinted that a dining room
Too imposing can cast a chill on a conversation

Of two or three friends, while a cozy nook
Can help it catch fire. And if the talk in the bungalow
Ever grew so expansive the walls couldn't hold it,
He could always, she might have added,
Usher his friends out back to the garden.

Now she worries that in keeping silent
She may have doomed him to learn the hard way
That princely spaces can't promise a princely destiny.
She has to hope he'd heard a proverb like that already,
Had sifted its truth, and found it wanting in spirit.

She has to hope he knew as well as she did
That projects are only wishes, each meant sincerely

As a climber means sincerely to avoid a rockslide,
As a balloonist means sincerely to cross an ocean
Till a fitful gust has the final say.

Ants

These ants busy under the picnic table
Where I sit tweaking my ode to summer
Descend from the same tribe that Solomon
Holds up as an example: "Go to the ant,
Thou sluggard, and be wise."
Is he speaking to me? Is he suggesting
I'm nowhere busy enough to suit him?
Look who's talking as he pens a proverb
While leaning back on his cushioned couch
In the grassy pergola of his summer palace.

It's far more likely he's addressing himself.
Another morning has been frittered away
In revising an invitation to the Queen of Sheba,
In adjusting the syntax and diction
So the sentences sound sincere,
Not like the usual courtly compliments.

"Go to the ant," he exhorts his majesty,
And as he writes he feels the crumbs
Of the poppy-seed cake he's nibbling
Fall from his glossy beard to the grass
Where the ants are waiting in silence.
Now for the long haul to the nest.
Now for packing the bulky load
In the bins allotted and falling asleep
In leather jerkins and work boots.

To go to the ants and decree their right
To be sluggards now and then
When the fancy takes them—
That would be an enterprise for a king.

Let them sleep in tomorrow while he succeeds
In drafting his invitation in an easy,
Holiday style, informal but earnest,
That Sheba needs to read only once
Before she orders her fleet to set sail.

Drugstore

Don't be ashamed that your parents
Didn't happen to meet at an art exhibit
Or at a protest against a foreign policy
Based on fear of negotiation,
But in an aisle of a discount drugstore,
Near the antihistamine section,
Seeking relief from the common cold.
You ought to be proud that even there,
Amid coughs and sneezes,
They were able to peer beneath
The veil of pointless happenstance.
Here is someone, each thought,
Able to laugh at the indignities
That flesh is heir to. Here
Is a person one might care about.
Not love at first sight, but the will
To be ready to endorse the feeling
Should it arise. Had they waited
For settings more promising,
You wouldn't be here,
Wishing things were different.
Why not delight at how young they were
When they made the most of their chances,
How young still, a little later,
When they bought a double plot
At the cemetery. Look at you,
Twice as old now as they were
When they made arrangements,
And still you're thinking of moving on,
Of finding a town with a climate
Friendlier to your many talents.
Don't be ashamed of the homely thought

That whatever you might do elsewhere
In the time remaining you might do here
If you can resolve, at last, to pay attention.

The Best World

Much about this edge of the park
May require little improvement to be included
In a scene from the best world.
The people strolling here under the branches
May bear a strong resemblance to strollers there
As they move along in pairs, trios, or tribes
Past benches like these. There too
Some enjoy circulating and some sitting still
And looking on. On the bench facing mine
The young man and two young women
Seem to be talking as easily as they would
On a bench in the best world, and the old man
Sitting alone with the paper is perusing the news
As eagerly as anyone would over there
Who has interests beyond the neighborhood.
And the middle-aged woman lost in a book
Wouldn't be out of place among those over there
Who believe their perspective could use some widening.
Only the entrance of a raggedy man
Jingling a paper cup might be a reminder
We're here, not there; for in the best world
Everyone has enough to live on.
Anyone begging there would be only pretending
To be a beggar, to give others the chance
To prove they were openhanded.
Now the woman, laying her book aside
To hunt in her purse, would be passing the test,
While the young man and his two friends,
Who don't look up, would be failing,
Unless they had pierced the beggar's disguise
And were vexed at having their kindness questioned.
Here in this park, where the beggar looks genuine,

The three may feel they deserve a rest
From workweek demands. Tomorrow, it may be hard
To tell their jobs from jobs in the best world
If they enjoy them as workers do over there,
Or as the two men I noticed an hour ago
Seemed to enjoy sharing a scaffold
As they washed the windows of an office building
Across from the park. How serene they looked,
As if they thought of themselves as privileged
To work far above the flow of traffic.
How could the best world be better for them
So long as they're pleased to witness an office
With grimy windows gradually brighten?
As for the people working inside, it's hard to say
If they're as grateful for their lighter spirits
As their counterparts would be in the best world.
Maybe some are, while others assume
They've only the wind to thank, the careless wind
That's happened to nudge a cloud away.

Mission to Ganymede

Even if Jupiter's biggest moon
Proves hostile to life in any form,
That's no reason to cancel plans
For an expedition. And if, after all the effort,
No one is any wiser about space or time,
Still the particulars of Ganymede's composition,
Topography, and climate may make the night sky
Seem closer to us by a mile or two.
As for a photo of Earth shot from Ganymede,
Who can say how moving the sight of that speck,
Outshone by a crowd of brighter neighbors,
Might appear to someone down here
When he comes across it in a magazine
In a waiting room on the fortieth floor
Of the Brisbane Building. Till now
He's been hankering for a job with a firm
Far grander than the firm he works for.
Now the image of his small planet,
Whose life is invisible from a distance,
Suggests that the interview then impending
Means less than it seemed to mean before.
Later, down on the street, when his glance
Falls on a clump of curbside burdock,
It may look to him like a green flag
Of a realm he ought to be serving as ardently
As others are serving Project Ganymede,
Which by then has taken five years of planning
And five of voyaging through ink-dark seas.
If he acts on his impulse, by the time the ship
Finally gets home, his backyard patch
Of tomato vines and bean rows
May have slowly burgeoned to become exemplary.

The book he'll have written on getting started
May be considered by many as one
Of the gospels of the gardening movement,
Along with its sequel proving a greenhouse
More practical in the long run than a garage.

Earth Day

"Mother Earth" is her name in fables,
But now we agree that the mothering
Needs to be done by the children
Whose reckless doings have aged her,
Creasing her brow, stooping her shoulders
As she's waited for them to return
From nights of drinking, from speeding
For thrills on icy roads.

A sad figure, but easier to confront
Than the facts of melting glaciers
And coastal flooding, of coral die-off
And dunes encroaching on settlements.
Compared to them, it isn't so hard
To imagine the house our mother waits in,
Once a mansion and now a ruin,
The roof rotted, the basement flooded,
The heirloom furniture pawned away
Piece by piece down to a rocking chair
Nobody wanted and a bed of straw.

Mother, I'm celebrating your day
By working as one of a volunteer crew
Walking the banks of Buffalo Creek with poles
To fish out tires and shopping carts,
Rugs, galoshes, and paint cans.
Let these be a sign of a pledge
Only a mother would trust
To undo our history.

But can we keep to the metaphor
When all mothers familiar to us

Are obliged to grow old? We're children
Hoping if we do our chores
An exception will be made in your case
So your back can straighten,
Your brow unfurrow, your hair, now gray,
Prove wheat-yellow once again.

Disgust

It isn't dependable as a guide when it flows
From a grudge against the body, but consider
How helpful it proved in prompting the god
Who revealed himself to the prophet Amos
To gag when he sniffed the savor rising
From temple altars. The smoke of sacrifice
Stank in his nostrils when the fires were lit
By those grown fat on the gleanings of orphans,
On bribes and kickbacks, on the plunder of war.

It couldn't have taken long for a god like that,
Made sick by sanctimonious prayer,
To lose his appetite completely
And dwindle to skin and bones.
No option then but abandoning heaven,
Leaving it to a deity with a stronger stomach.

Down here, he'd have been likely to choose
A rural retreat for his retirement,
Where people worshipped only the gods of harvest:
Potato god, corn god, rain god, sun god.
He couldn't object to simple prayers for continuance,
To a faith in what he considered his best work:
The first five days of creation.

Maybe in time he chose to live on the land
Himself and serve the seasons, to be a farmer
Not too proud to sell his produce on weekends
From a stand at the end of his driveway.
Here come the city-dwellers who prefer to buy
From local growers. Good for them
If they're not put off by the smell of the barnyard

Or by the mud the farmer's left on the roots,
Enough for a grub to hide in, or an earthworm.

While they drive home to a homely meal,
He piles his boxes back on his truck,
Exhorting himself not to feel disgust when comparing
The garden he first conceived for the planet
With the gardens he's willing to sponsor now.

Cougar

Now that the few big questions with fangs and claws
That used to roam the uplands of conversation
Have dwindled away or been driven off,
It's no surprise that the population of little questions
Has multiplied till the woods and meadows
Are threatened with overgrazing, the spring shoots
Chewed down to the nub, the bark stripped
From the boles of the doomed saplings.
One fierce question like "Why are you starving
Your soul while you feed your flesh on dainties?"
Could keep in check the crowd of inquiries
Now pressing in about filling the gap
Between lunch and dinner on a rainy Sunday.
Do you want to watch a movie about Hawaii?
Do you want to put up shelving in the garage
So you'll be able to find the bag of charcoal
When it's time for a backyard barbecue?
No more tracks in the mud of a wolf or cougar
That made a walk to the barn an adventure.
No letter to be read by candlelight in the kitchen
At the plank table from Great-Uncle Obadiah
Who wants to know if you're doing something at last
To justify your existence, to prove,
Despite appearances, that the gift of life
Wasn't thrown away when it dropped on you.

After the Second Flood

At first, the last two men in the world,
Oscar and Omar, want to live side by side
For the sake of company. But soon
The sound of Omar's tinkering with his car,
As if with the right adjustment
It could run on air, makes Oscar gloomy.
And the sound of Oscar's dragging his trash
To the curb on what was trash day,
As if the ghosts of trash collectors gone by
Would soon be pulling up in their truck,
Puts Omar on edge. So they sign a contract
Dividing the planet neatly between them,
One hemisphere for each, and add a clause
Stipulating a coin toss if neither party
Is willing to move south.

It doesn't take long till Omar decides
That his half, with its many swamps
And deserts, is clearly the lesser one.
Not long till it's clear to Oscar
That the extra time he devotes to gardening
Earns him the right to extra land
From Omar's unworked portion.

If neither budges, and they both
Want to be justified in the eyes of the world,
The world of one plus one,
Their only recourse is to go to law,
Bringing their case before the bench

Of judges Oscar and Omar,
Who pledge themselves to allow
No apparent conflict of interest
To warp their judgment.

It will be a real workout for them
As they play the parts of all the witnesses
And file all the motions and counter-motions
For the attorneys who can't be present.
Objection, Your Honors; objection sustained.
So goes the drama, as the sergeant at arms,
Acted in tandem by Oscar and Omar,
Hushes the gallery, empty except for them,
When a clerk announces
A ruling from the court may be expected
In the near future but not today.

The Mood

It's only sensible for me to want to flourish
In mind and heart and body, but why
Should I want you to flourish as well
Unless I believe it's in my interest?
Why should I put myself out for your sake
When I'm not in the mood, when my body
Wants to sleep in, my heart
Isn't moved by the thought of your company,
And my mind considers your mind conventional?
Find someone else to drive you
To the repair shop to pick up your car.
As for the famous injunction you hint at,
"Love your neighbor as yourself,"
If it made any sense, would its big promoters
Be obliged to have it repeated each week
From millions of pulpits? Would it require
More than a dozen gods to endorse it,
Ghostly no-shows I'm not in the mood to please?
Let others compete for the prize reserved
For a will always generous while I watch
From the viewing stand or turn away.
Bad moods, my Aunt Celia said,
In a burst of metaphor, fifty years ago,
When she thought I hadn't helped with cleanup
In the proper spirit, are clouds
Clustering low on a mountain, while the peak,
Rising above them, basks in the sun.
But what about clouds that bump the sky?
Aunt Celia, who told me not to be moody
When the oldsters at dinner turned the talk
To their pains and illnesses, away from the movie
I wanted to ask about. That's just their way,

She suggested, of reminding themselves
How little time they have left for a final proof
They haven't been living by bread alone.
And what exactly, she asked, did I suppose
I was living for? Just for pleasure?
Couldn't a boy endowed with ambition
Come up with a project larger than that?
But if I have, it doesn't include
Driving you anywhere, not today,
Not in this mood I've explained enough.

Outdoor Café

The odds I'll climb Mount Everest
At least once in the years still left me
Are long, but not so long as the odds
I'll sit alone at least once all afternoon
At this café table without a book
Or newspaper for company
Or without a pen and notebook to help me
Arrange my thoughts in a sequence.

No book or paper, and no expectation
A friend will be joining me later on.
Just the silent acceptance of life
As it flows in the talk around me.
What an endless tundra to cross alone
While up at the camp in the mountains
My two Sherpas are making breakfast.
Soon we'll be breaking bread together
Before we gather our gear for the summit.

Look there, at that high glint in the east,
They'll say, pointing. But in this café
It will take a miracle for me to choose
To sit alone with the bare moment.
A miracle to believe this puff of wind
Flapping the awning above me
Has come on purpose just to be here,
Here where it would surely settle
If allowed more options than moving on.

An English Teacher

If we're only the sum of the roles we play,
He's a lucky man, it seems to him,
To be able to earn his living playing a role
That has him standing in front of a class
With a book in his hand that deserves attention.
He's at his best then, he feels,
Furthest from the drone of the question
Of whether he's getting enough at the feast of life,
Whether others are being served more zealously.
As long as he faces his students, he can hold his focus
On helping them to admire a work of art
As much as he does. Not till he's home
Does he find himself lapsing into the role of a man
Who regards his talents as flowers too fine
To thrive in the thin soil he's been allotted.
And even then he can sometimes shake off
The postures of melodrama if a stack of papers
Exhorts him to practice the art of grading.
Time to find out how well his students have managed
To explain the use of the double plot in *King Lear*
Or the logic of metaphors in "Ode to Autumn."
While he fills the margins, he tries not to ask
If those who read his comments will understand
He isn't trying to shake their confidence
But to make them critics. To play that role
They'll have to move past private associations
And learn the art of forgetting themselves,
The art the authors practiced when they turned
From the breakfast table and morning paper
To sit at their desks and write of a world
Larger than any visible from their study windows,
Though a swarm of gnats by a sweetgum tree

Or a driving cloud may have set them musing.
Once they began, he'll tell his students,
They embraced the role of a traveler
Who hasn't a map to guide him,
Who can't be sure he's walking a road
That leads where he's hoping to go
Until he follows it to the end.

Praise

Good for those who visit your hospital room
Because the chore comes with their job
And they want to be conscientious.
And good for those who sit by your bed
And lean forward to listen
Because they're resolved to practice
Rule One in the book of courtesy:
To act as if what the speaker says
Interests them deeply, whatever feelings
May be flowing through them.
And don't forget those who, having promised
To read you a book, plunge in on their next visit
Because they consider a promise binding.
And here's to the one or two who'd be insulted
If you asked them to promise,
Aggrieved by the intimation you thought their resolve
Had to be propped in place by a pledge.
For them a promise is a rickety footbridge
Over a river prone to flooding,
While intention is safe in the shelter
Of a single soul, a soul you should try
To imagine rowing across in its little boat,
High water or low, to the wharf
On the other side where the bus stops
That goes to the hospital. Here it comes now,
And here is the window seat
Where the riders can unwrap their sandwiches
As they ponder questions to ask you
About your illness, the choices of treatment,
The stages you'll have to move through
Before a complete recovery. And now
As the bus leaves the river valley behind

And climbs into hills, imagine these riders
Prompted to think of subjects stretching
Beyond you to the horizon, vistas
They want to believe you're waiting for.

Tattoo

If the body is the house of the soul,
What's wrong with a little home decoration
More permanent than the drapes in the parlor
Or the fabric on the dining-room chairs?

A forearm, say, adorned with a tropical flower
Or with a palm tree under a deep blue sky,
Suggesting the body is glad to recall
Its stay in Eden, whether or not the soul
Regards that episode as relevant now.

Or consider the young waitress
Who served you lunch just an hour ago,
How her sleeveless blouse revealed
A small heart on her shoulder
Inscribed with two names, Dave and Gretchen,
Under a sprig of lilac.

No need to assume she's failed to imagine a time
When a boyfriend more congenial
Wakes up beside her only to be reminded
There was once a Dave who was all she wanted.

Could be she wants to send a reminder
To the Gretchen she may become
Not to forget the girl who believed
That holding on was a project worthy
Of all the attention that she could muster,
As much a challenge as letting go.

Belittle

"Belittle" was one of the words we coined
When we were still colonials to help us
Shrug off critiques of our ambitions.
Who cares if our English cousins belittled Franklin
For his youthful program of self-improvement,
If the virtues he chose to make his own
Seem more appropriate to a tradesman
Than to a hero. Yes, his weekly grades suggest
He considered the soul as something achieved
Through extra homework. But at least he was willing
To acknowledge he wasn't the man he hoped to be.
And while he charted his private progress,
He found time at meetings of the club he founded
To share with his fellow journeymen his notions
For improving the streets, the schools,
The fire departments, the hospitals.
And why not a lending library so men of spirit
Who wore leather aprons during the workday
Could sit at a table all evening and learn
All they needed to be the equal of gentlemen
In judging the soundness of any policy?
How belittling he considered it to be told
Governors enjoyed a conduit to the truth
Common folk were cut off from.
How belittling he would find it now
To be assured by our leaders that our enemies
Hate us for our love of freedom and justice,
Not for any wrong we may have done them.
To admit even one failure of tact
Is a step that ought not to be belittled
If it leads to the kind of improvement that Franklin made.
We'll need to examine our motives more closely

If we belittle him for selling his printing house
When scarcely middle-aged to devote himself
Full time to public service. Instead of mocking
His hope of making a difference, it behooves us
To cheer it on. So what if he fails to persuade
His Majesty's government to be friendlier
To her colonies. So what if his success
With the French depends far less on his skill
In negotiation than on the grudges the Court
Bears toward the English. How small of us
If we belittle him on his voyage home,
His tours of duty finally behind him,
When he vows to give the rest of his life to science,
A man in his eighties assuming he can resume
A passion he set aside forty years before.
There he goes, hobbling from his cabin,
When his gout and gallstones allow it,
To measure the temperature of the Gulf Stream.
How unfair it would be to fault his project
Merely because the people of Pennsylvania,
As soon as he steps ashore,
Prevail on him to become their president
And send him later to help with the Constitution.
We ought to defend him when he drowses off
During the longer speeches to dream
Of the laboratory he planned to add to his house
And the many experiments that might have proven
The end of life not constrained by what comes before.

Instructions from Lucy in Elmira

Now that my editor here at the *Beacon*
Has again promoted someone else to the job
I wanted, it's time for you to assure me
He's made the mistake he always makes:
Preferring charm over substance.

Now your task is to say that the pain I feel
Is evidence that I still believe
Justice is possible, that I haven't succumbed
To the notion pushed by the skeptical
And ironical that nobody ever changes,
Nobody learns what he needs to learn.

And don't forget to predict that soon
I'll be glad I wasn't assigned to write
Accounts of the lives of the famous and fortunate,
Glad I'm allowed to keep my focus
On the obscure and modest, whose obituaries
Call for deeper reserves of imagination.

I'm sending you here my article on Ellen Tucker,
Our late librarian. Read it and tell me
How it captures a truth useful for anyone
Interested in imagining what it must have been like
Growing up in Elmira, in the thirties and forties,
On elm-canopied River Street as a bookish girl
Doted on by her parents, a nurse and a pharmacist.

Then persuade me my article leaves its readers
Sorry they never asked for her help
In guiding their reading, never heard her theory
That history books should be read as stories

Of lives the readers themselves have lived
In other places and other times.

Tell me I'm following her advice
By wondering, when I think of her,
Why it was that words that had no effect
When spoken by others
Pierced to the heart when she spoke them.
Tell me you think that maybe one day
Someone might say the same of me.

Then write the *Beacon* to say my articles
Prove that it's possible here in Elmira
To escape the narrowness of the provinces,
Though the *Beacon* at times may suggest the opposite.
I'm trying to take my cue from Ellen Tucker,
Who cast her mustard seeds where she could
And didn't presume to guess if the soil
Was soft or stony, deep or thin.

On the Train to Florida

I can believe the man in the seat facing mine
When he tells me he's traveling to a reunion
Of five shipmates who rented a launch
In Key Largo six years ago.

But when he adds they pushed off from the dock
On a mercy mission, intent on reaching the prison
Beyond the laws of the mainland, I'm skeptical.
Chances are he's making the story up to suggest

He's a man of principle, not merely convinced
That everyone, guilty or innocent, deserves a trial,
But willing to bring that belief from the couch
Of thought to the ebb and swell of action.

But why would he care whether someone like me,
Who's nothing to him, admires his enterprise,
A stranger reading a book on the Everglades
On a train ride south for a nephew's graduation?

And if self-promotion were really his motive,
Why admit that twenty miles into their voyage
The Coast Guard boarded their boat
And steered it back to the dock they'd left from.

So much for their plan to enter the harbor at dawn
And dispel the rumor among the prisoners
That out of sight meant out of mind.
And would a boaster laugh at himself

For the music he claims they were planning
To play on deck, the fanfares

They hoped might wake one guard
From a dream of empire and send him scurrying

Down a corridor to unlock a cell?
"Five crazies," he calls his outfit, while admitting
They proved too sane for a second try.
"A story hard to believe," he says in summary,

As if guessing my reservations, and then
Goes on to admit that he and his friends
Might not believe the story themselves
If they didn't meet once a year

To assure themselves that it really happened.
It's fine with him, he assures me,
If I suppose he only dreamed it,
So long as I'm sorry I can't believe.

A Word from the Sleepless

If you were troubled like us, the sleepless,
You too would try to comfort yourself with numbers,
Seeking out symptoms of your affliction
Among the many who appear rested.
You too would try to interpret the walk
A neighbor takes just before dawn
Less as a sign that he's eager for morning
Than as a technique to tire himself by nightfall,
To meet the god of sleep more than halfway.

Like us, you'd regard the work of the town reformer,
Valuable as it is, as only partly prompted
By civic concern, by his resolve, say, to make the river
Safe again for swimming and fishing. You too
Would suspect that one of his motives is private:
To throw a bone to his watchdog conscience
For doings he's not so proud of.
May it not bark tonight, he prays,
And block the gate to the house of dream.

We admire as much as you do the colleague
Who refuses to answer with spite the spiteful words
Of those who attack her causes
By attacking her character. Still, don't you agree
That the adjective "wise" describes her
Better than "saintly"? Here's someone who's learned
That if she gets into bed nursing a grudge
And plotting revenge, she'll shorten her stay
By many hours in a realm more peaceable.

If you'd like an example of real saintliness,
Think of someone who calmly watches

As you sail off to the fabled realm of sleep
In a breeze that never falters.
The one who waves from the dock
With barely a trace of resentment
As the yacht others deserve as much as you do
Slowly grows small and disappears.

Anthropology

Soft hollows in the clay, a few feet beneath the surface,
With a half-inch layer of bone dust at the bottom,
Suggest that some of the creatures who lived here
Buried their dead, a supposition that's strengthened
If you happen to find a stone like this one
That looks to have been scratched by a digging tool.
Thousands of years ago the wooden shaft
Crumbled away, carved in all likelihood with an image
Of a snake or turtle, fox or bear.
It comforted the digger to be reminded
The tribe wasn't alone, that it had its own
Particular woodland kin always at hand
In times of trial. A fox or bear
To stand guard at a grave newly dug, a turtle
To lead a spirit down to its ancestors.
Does it make you sad to think of the trust
They placed in folkways founded on hope alone,
Not on reliable information? Would you be happier
If they'd been more skeptical, like you, like me?
Maybe as spirits they pestered their guide with questions
As they followed, stumbling, in the dark.
Why, for starters, hadn't their forebears
Visited them more often in dreams
To share their wisdom? Did they try and fail,
Finding the uphill journey too daunting?
Or do the hardships the living face
Seem sand-grain small when viewed
From the far place where the dead dwell?
Or is time the problem, long years above
Only an eyeblink to those below?
Be patient, is all the turtle says.
Soon you will know what I know, if not more.

One Future

If you're right that only one future
Can follow from this particular present,
Then my listing of pros and cons on the legal pad
Here at this desk in my attic study—
The windows shut, the curtains drawn
Against distraction—is irrelevant,
A pretense that I'm in charge of the dinghy
Being swept to sea by an irresistible tide.
But isn't talk of a tide more suited
To spells of sweeping passion
Than to the work of slowly climbing
At least some part of the path to the bluff
Overlooking the bay? Down below,
The map of my habits, partly obscured
By mist or cloud, lies unfolded,
The predictable pattern of thought that led
To predictable errors I've learned to evade
Or compensate for with strategies
Tested and modified over decades.
I've written my angry letter to the editor
Exposing the plot of the town board
To favor private schools over public,
But I haven't sent it, and won't
Till I've read it again in a calmer moment.
And here is my letter to a possible friend
Stating more than I feel in the hope that one day
I can make it true. And here is my letter
Stating less, which may be more honest,
Given my history. Maybe you're right
That the one I send is already recorded
In invisible ink in the diary of tomorrow.
But what if a feather's weight

Dropped on the lighter side of the scale
Would tip the balance, the weight,
Say, of a phone call from you
Offering me an argument I've neglected?
If you dial my number, you can argue
You had to do it, given all you are.
If you fail to call, you can say the same.
Meanwhile, the question you face
Is who is the person you'd prefer to emerge
At the end of the chain of causes
Now working unseen beneath the surface.
Is it someone destined to withhold advice
For fear he may be mistaken
And held responsible? Is it someone
Destined to disclose what he thinks he'd do
In a similar situation, or, better yet,
What he'd want to do if he were free?

Devising Scripture

Now that archeologists can agree
That the fall of Jericho is a fiction
(The walls not breached, the houses not burned),
We can hope the same for the painful passage
About the Amelekites, how the tribe is slaughtered
On Yahweh's orders, as Samuel reports them,
"Men and women, children and little babies,"
Put to the sword without a tear.
Maybe this story too was added by priests
Long after the kingdom was a going concern
To give more drama to its prosy origins.
Not for them the facts of a scruffy settlement
In the hills of Canaan whose neighbors sometimes
Exhausted each other with endless skirmishing.

It takes a while for the word "neighbor"—
As in "Love thy neighbor"—to apply to a tribe
Different from yours. Till then, it simply refers
To somebody down the street weaker than you are.
Here comes the prophet Nathan, a few chapters on,
To inform King David he's offended heaven
By seizing Uriah's wife, Bathsheba,
By ordering that her husband, a loyal captain,
Be abandoned on the battlefield by generals
Obedient to their chief, not to the Law.
Here's David pierced by the justice
Of Nathan's words, however painful.
Yes, he's the rich man in the prophet's parable
Who seizes the poor man's one pet lambkin.

If that episode is fiction too, whoever wrote it
Deserves to feel some pride in his handiwork

As he walks home from the house of scribes,
Though maybe as he nears his own street
His pride is chastened. It isn't easy for him
To be as pleased with himself as he wants to be
When down the block from his family
Lives a woman he has to work to resist,
Who makes Bathsheba seem dull and blowsy,
Whose husband, compared to bright Uriah,
Is a patch of darkness.

"What's for dinner?" our author asks
In a cheery voice, but his wife is fretful.
It seems their daughter has again neglected
Her carding and spinning to draw water
For strangers—servants as well as masters—
And for all their camels.
"How long," the father shouts at the girl,
"Do you think our well will serve our family
If you insist on quenching the thirst of the world?"

Still, as he shouts, a reedy voice
Whispers to him he ought to be proud
He has a daughter naturally generous.
And two days later, that's the very voice
He chooses to listen to when he's requested
To add an episode to a chapter in Genesis
In which Rebecca proves, unawares,
She's the right woman for gentle Isaac.
All at once a scene at her father's well
Floats into the writer's daydream
As he sits alone during a quiet interval
When the louder voices are resting.

A Motel Keeper

It isn't his busy season, so when a car
Breaks down a mile from his motel
He's glad to offer the elderly couple
A room at a special discount—
Three nights for the price of one.
Let the two wait in comfort for the broken part
To arrive at the local repair shop.

Maybe this gesture can compensate
For what he knows might well have happened
If they'd been stranded here two months ago
When every room could be rented at market value.
Then he'd have seemed to them another example
Of somebody bent on laying up treasure on earth
For himself and his few familiars.

His task now isn't to tell them a truth
That might make them hesitate but to act
As a generous man might act, eager
To confer a gift of leisure unlooked for.
Let him be glad if the rain lets up
And they have a chance to explore
Spots of notable local beauty easy to reach
On foot in the crisp air of late October.

Now to watch with pleasure as they stride off.
Now to hope that the spring in their step
Is more substantial, more telling,
Than the slouch of the ghostly unfortunates
They might have been not long ago
As they sat in his lobby,
A phone book between them,
Calling about a room in a town nearby.

Recall Notice

Gone now the young professor
Who took pleasure in hauling Lear
Before the court of a sophomore classroom
And pronouncing the old king headstrong,
Hungry for praise, intemperate,
And flagrantly ignorant of the world,
Confident he can cede his kingdom
And still retain his kingly authority.

Gone the old professor the young one became,
Who taught that Lear deserves to be praised,
After the arrogance of Act One,
For shaking his fist in the face of calamity
And asking what can be made
Of the nothing he's left with,
Or the next-to-nothing.

Gone the students taught the old view,
Whose notebooks the old professor
Would have liked to recall for some serious
Alterations in focus and tone.
Or if not the notebooks of all,
Then those of the few who paid attention
And remembered the class long afterward.
Rebecca Bryce, for instance,
Who sat near the front, head bent,
Taking every word down,
While most of the others studied the rain
Soaking the hemlocks outside the window.

To her he'd have been happy to send a note
Expressing the hope no lecture of his

Berating Lear for trusting in flattery
Left her suspicious of friendly overtures,
Reluctant to let her guard down for a minute.
To her a note hoping his pious praise
Of Lear's belated humility and contrition
Didn't induce her to suffer injustice tamely.

Gone from the world the belief that the two
Can talk about it in some other life,
A life that now only imagination
Finds room for. There he's delighted
To learn from her that his worry
Is more than a little ridiculous,
His claim to an influence
He never came close to possessing.

There he has a chance to be foolish,
Like Lear at the end,
Oblivious to the issue of royal authority.
And after the end, when the king
Chats over there with Cordelia all afternoon,
The professor makes sure that the pair
Are not interrupted. There he goes,
Patrolling the perimeter of their country cottage,
Turning messengers from the Court away.

To the Angel of Death

I'll admit you've a steady hand if you'll admit
Any hope you may have nursed at the outset
Of having your work respected
As well as feared has come to nothing.

Had you made a good-faith effort to explain
Your apparent indifference to the harm you do,
You might have earned some credit. Your silence,
However, suggests you believe your reasons

Far beyond our ken. Or else you've abandoned
All hope of understanding your own procedures,
Of learning the implications behind the names
Presented to you each morning for blotting out.

Habit—that's most likely what moves you now,
And the dim notion that your superiors,
Who never stoop to explain themselves,
Know what they're doing.

While they issue commands, you stand before them
Shuffling your feet, head bowed,
Nervously folding and unfolding your wings;
And then, dismissed, you ape your masters

By refusing to listen to us. Are you hoping
Your truckling will one day earn you
An invitation to join their inner council?
Or is it enough for you to stand where you are,

Close enough to power to borrow its luster?
All that glinting, but never a dawning insight
About how little you mean to those you work for,
How our objections should be yours as well.

More Poetry

When he read of a woman in a village
Fifty miles south of Tehran
Teaching English to her high-school class
By teaching Whitman, my friend Herbert
Decided to lead an online discussion group
On Iranian poetry. True, he knew little
About the subject; but having been moved
By her conviction that it's hard to spurn
A nation when you know its poets,
He wanted to make the subject his own.

Ignorant, yes, but prompt to admit it
And invite those who knew more
To be generous, once a week, with suggestions;
Grateful if someone helped with a stubborn passage
By offering a translation truer to the original
Than the one in the book he'd chosen.
What had seemed a boulder blocking the path
Suddenly proved a bush whose comely flowers
Travelers paused to admire awhile
Before they stepped around it and moved on.

Even now he presides every week for two hours
Of steady progress. And when he turns from the screen,
He devotes an hour to imagining what went on
That day in the village classroom.
"Can anyone tell me," he can hear the woman asking,
"What the word 'limitless' means in Whitman's lines,
'And limitless are leaves stiff or drooping in the fields
And brown ants in the little wells beneath them'?

Is he saying simply 'too many to count'
Or something bolder and farther reaching?"

And if some students conclude it means "priceless"
To those who are free enough to see
The low as lofty, the last as first,
While others are sure it means "wholly beyond
Our limited human understanding,"
She doesn't push for consensus.
"Whitman would likely be happy," she tells them,
"With either answer. But to take the two
As two twigs leafing out on a tree
Outside our window might please him more."

Last Interview

Would you say, looking back, that one moment
Proved defining, breaking your life
Into before and after, a dark age
Followed by an enlightenment?
Or has your development been more gradual,
A slow-growing commitment, say, to ferry
The light of truth, as it dawned for you, into darkness,
Now making headway against contrary currents,
Now falling back? Did you find the work lonely,
Or did you glimpse a flicker answering yours
And steer in its direction through lingering mist?
Was the meeting a joyful one? Did it end
With a shared promise to keep in touch?
Would you say the thought of the good you were doing
In teaching, for instance, a class in prison
Made the long drive easy? Or did you need
Some help from the scenery, from a question
Like whether an old church by a filling station
Was beautiful still despite the wound
Dealt to its symmetry by the new brick annex?
Were you ever forced to pull off the road
When you suddenly realized that your feelings
For a woman you considered simply a friend
Had a will of their own and an agenda?
Did you yield to their entreaties or resist them
To save your strength for ventures to come?
As for the trips you planned to take but didn't,
Do you blame bad luck, when blaming feels essential,
Or a change of heart? Have you fought fire
With fire, a destructive passion like spite
With a creative one like indignation,
Or have you tried to immerse all flame

In a deep pool of quiet and emerge serene,
With a sheaf of blessings you bound yourself?
Have you blessings left to scatter on likely soil?
On the whitewashed wall above your desk,
Do the figures depicted in the reproduction
Look as if they will live forever
Or as if they will die one day, and know it?
Can you tell us about the day you understood
That the tree destined to shade your grave
Was already tall, that the shovel handle
Was already fitted into the steel socket?
Did the resolutions you made then
Suffer more, when they proved unworkable,
From a want of will or a want of focus?
Do you think your focus would have been more clear
If you'd asked yourself what we're asking now?

Carl Dennis is the author of ten previous works of poetry and a collection of essays, *Poetry as Persuasion*. A recipient of the Pulitzer Prize and the Ruth Lilly Prize, he lives in Buffalo, New York.

PENGUIN POETS